KING CHARLES III
GREAT LIVES IN GRAPHICS

Button
BOOKS

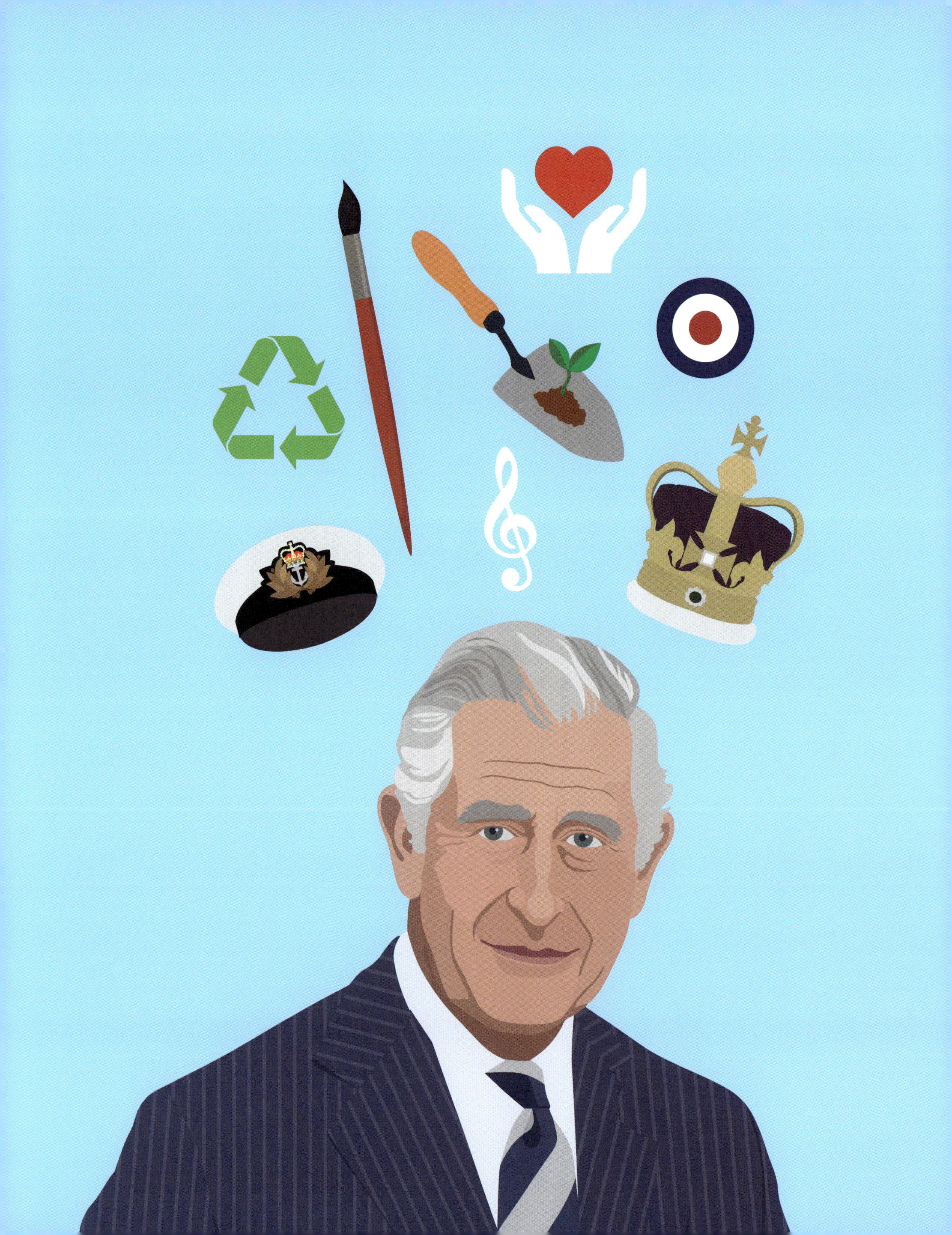

Charles III is a king of many talents. He was the first heir to the throne to get a university degree, can fly jets and helicopters, plays piano, cello and trumpet, and is a best-selling children's author.

He's also been a pioneer in the campaign against climate change, has founded 18 charities and built his own town.

His life so far has been one of highs, lows, challenges and triumphs. It's the story of a modern man who is now the head of an ancient institution, and set to claim a unique place in British history. To find out how, why, and more besides, read on…

Life & times of CHARLES III

1948
Charles Philip Arthur George Mountbatten-Windsor is born on 14 November at Buckingham Palace

1954
Food rationing ends in the UK

1961
World Wildlife Fund (WWF) established

1963
Martin Luther King Jr makes his 'I Have a Dream' speech

1965
US scientists voice concerns about the 'greenhouse effect'

1969
Charles invested Prince of Wales at Caernarfon Castle

1972
Gene Cernan, commander of Apollo 17, becomes the last human to walk on the moon

1977
Star Wars is released in cinemas

1981
Charles marries Lady Diana Spencer at St Paul's Cathedral, London

1982
Charles and Diana's son William is born

1983
First mobile phone goes on sale

1984
Charles and Diana's second son Prince Henry (known as Harry) born

1990
Nelson Mandela released from prison

1994
Season one of Friends released

1997
Diana, Princess of Wales, dies

2005
Charles marries Camilla Parker Bowles

2007
Seventh and final Harry Potter book published

2018
Eco-activist Greta Thunberg goes on her first school strike

2020
Worldwide coronavirus pandemic

2022
Queen Elizabeth II, Charles's mother dies

2023
Charles crowned king of the United Kingdom

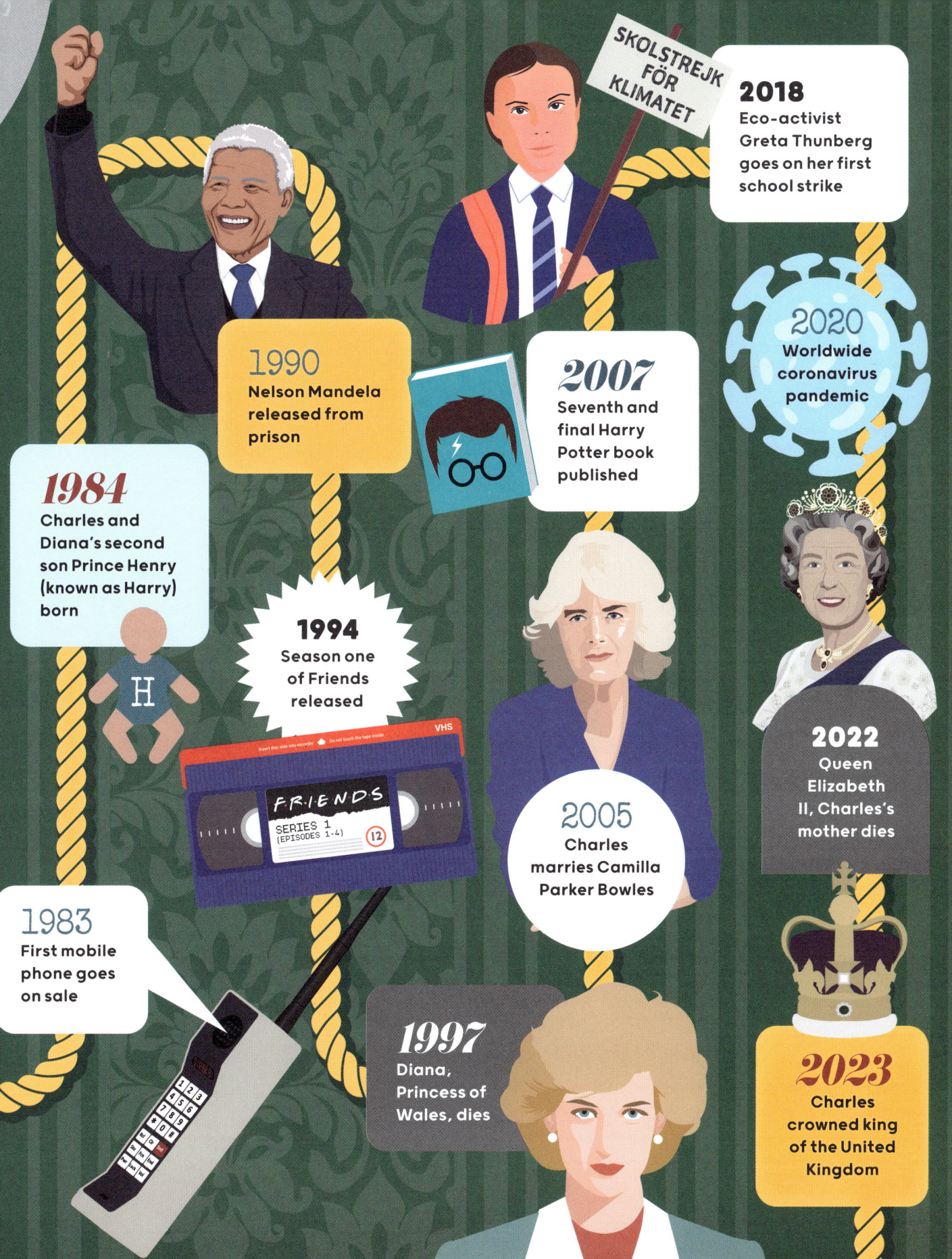

CERTIFIED COPY OF AN ENTRY
Pursuant to the Births and Deaths Registration Act 1953

NAME
CHARLES PHILIP ARTHUR GEORGE MOUNTBATTEN-WINDSOR

BIRTH DATE
14 NOVEMBER 1948

WHERE
BUCKINGHAM PALACE

WEIGHT
7LB 6OZ

PRINCE PHILIP PLAYED SQUASH while his wife Princess Elizabeth was in labour with Charles. At the time, fathers were not usually present at the birth of their children.

Charles's birth was the **FIRST** of a senior member of the Royal Family **NOT** to be **WITNESSED BY A POLITICIAN** for centuries. This tradition went back to the 17th century. It was done to ensure the child was a genuine descendant of the monarch.

BORN TO RULE

OKAY BOOMER! The King is a **BABY BOOMER**, one of a generation of people born between **1946** and **1964**, a period after World War II that saw an increase in births.

BRITAIN IN 1948

BRITISH EMPIRE
George VI ruled over hundreds of millions of people in territories across the world but the empire was in decline.

RATIONS
Three years after World War II, meat, cheese, butter, margarine, sugar, milk and eggs were all controlled and given out in small quantities to the British people.

CRIME WAVE
BETWEEN 1938 AND 1948, THE CRIME RATE DOUBLED

FORCES
1.5 MILLION BRITS were serving in the Army, Navy or Royal Air Force.

FAMILY ALBUM

EDWARD VIII
Abdicated (that is, he gave up the throne) 1936
1894 - 1972

Great Uncle

TWO NANNIES
Charles' nannies were Helen Lightbody and Mabel Anderson. They taught him to walk, talk and play. He later called Mabel, 'the great haven'.

FOUR HOMES
The British Royal Family has many residencies...

BALMORAL
Scotland

> "THE BEST PLACE ON EARTH"
> King Charles III

QUEEN ELIZABETH
(later Queen Elizabeth The Queen Mother)
1900 - 2002

Grandmother

GEORGE VI
1895 - 1952

Grandfather

SANDRINGHAM
Norfolk

WINDSOR CASTLE
Berkshire

BUCKINGHAM PALACE
London

PRINCESS ELIZABETH
(later Elizabeth II)
1926 - 2022

Mother

PHILIP MOUNTBATTEN
(later Prince Philip, Duke of Edinburgh)
1921 - 2021

Father

> 'I WANT HIM TO BE A MAN'S MAN'
>
> A reported quote from Prince Philip, who taught his son to
>
> SWIM   SHOOT   FISH

CHARLES
1948 -

ANNE
1950 -

Sister

ANDREW
1960 -

Brother

EDWARD
1964 -

Brother

'IT'S SUCH A HOLE

AGE 5-8

In 1956, just before his eighth birthday, Charles went to school in London, and six years later, he moved on to Gordonstoun. **HE WAS NOT A HAPPY SCHOOLBOY**, and here's why…

Charles was taught boxing and wrestling before he went to school.

Before starting school he was educated by a governess called 'Mipsy' at Buckingham Palace.

His grandmother, the Queen Mother, taught him the history of the Royal Family and encouraged his love of music and art.

In the Spring of 1957, Charles had his **tonsils removed** and, for a few months after, insisted on taking them with him in a jar wherever he went.

AGE 8-13

After attending Hill House school in West London for a few months, Charles went to **CHEAM SCHOOL, BERKSHIRE** as a boarder (i.e. he lived there and only went home during holidays). His father, Prince Philip went there too. He said…

'…SCHOOL IS EXPECTED TO BE A SPARTAN AND DISCIPLINED EXPERIENCE'

 Charles was beaten by the headmaster for bullying another boy!

He played cricket and rugby, acted in a school play and, in his fifth year there, was made Head Boy, but has said he 'loathed' his time at Cheam School.

THIS PLACE!"

Charles's education was unlike that of any heir to the British throne before him....

AGE 13-18

Many people thought Charles would go to Eton College, the elite senior school founded by Henry VI in 1440.

Instead, he was sent to his father's old school, **GORDONSTOUN** in Scotland, because it was far away from nosey journalists based in London.

GORDONSTOUN SCHOOL

NOSEY JOURNALISTS

Every morning, all pupils went for a **MORNING RUN** and had a **COLD SHOWER** before breakfast.

Charles slept in a wooden hut with the windows open, alongside 14 other boys.

'I SIMPLY DREAD GOING TO BED AS I GET HIT ALL NIGHT LONG...'

As an adult, Charles has said Gordonstoun helped in his development but at the time he described it as a 'prison sentence'.

OFF TO UNI!

In 1967, Charles went to **TRINITY COLLEGE, CAMBRIDGE**

First heir to the throne to earn a university degree

He studied **ARCHAEOLOGY ANTHROPOLOGY HISTORY**

PLAYED POLO

ENJOYED SHOOTING

ACTED IN PLAYS

During his time at Cambridge, a police detective did his laundry to guard against fans stealing his clothes.

Charles did not receive his degree in person because it was feared that might provoke hostile demonstrations.

Prince of Wales

The Queen made Charles Prince of Wales when he was nine years old. Later, during his student days, the Prince spent three months at the University College of Wales in Aberystwyth, ahead of his investiture in 1969

For & against

Charles received a generally warm welcome in Aberystwyth but not everyone was pleased to see him. Welsh nationalists, in particular, were not happy about the prince's short stay in his principality.

Welsh nationalism

Nationalists want Wales to be an independent country that governs itself and is separate from the rest of the United Kingdom.

Founded in 1925, the political party Plaid Cymru (Party of Wales) works to protect and promote the country, its language and its traditions.

'EVERY DAY I HAD TO GO DOWN TO THE TOWN WHERE I WENT TO THESE LECTURES, AND MOST DAYS THERE SEEMED TO BE A DEMONSTRATION GOING ON AGAINST ME.'

CHARLES ON HIS TIME IN ABERYSTWYTH

NOT MY KING, NOT MY PRINCE

WELCOME! TO HIS ROYAL HIGHNESS

Learning the lingo

Over nine weeks, Charles was taught Welsh by Edward Milward, a member of Plaid Cymru, who refused to address him with any title other than 'Mr'.

The Prince learnt enough to make his first public speech in Welsh at the Urdd National Eisteddfod (the annual Welsh youth festival of poetry, drama and music). There were some protests, but the speech was well received by most of the crowd.

'TYWYSOG CYMRU'
(Prince of Wales in Welsh)

CHECK THIS OUT

Prince of Wales check is a fabric pattern popularised by Edward VII when he was the Prince and taken on by his successor, the future Edward VIII. The pattern of small and large checks is actually Scottish and dates to the 19th century.

Investiture

★ On 1 July 1969, Queen Elizabeth invested her son Charles as Prince of Wales at Caernarfon Castle.

★ Around 3,000 troops lined the route and served as a guard of honour.

★ Fears that nationalists such as the Free Wales Army might disrupt the ceremony came to nothing.

★ The ceremony did not include any reference to the fact that Wales had once been an independent nation.

★ During this televised event, the Queen, Prince Philip and Charles all sat on thrones made of Welsh slate.

WHAT'S IN A WORD?

INVESTITURE

This is a formal ceremony at which a person is invested with (given) an official title, rank or honour.

A VERY QUICK HISTORY OF THE P.O.W

✱ The first Prince of Wales was the future Edward II who was invested in 1301. His father Edward I had conquered Wales in 1283.

✱ The title is only given to the heir to the British throne.

✱ The Prince's heraldic badge of three ostrich feathers, a coronet and the German motto 'Ich dien' ('I serve') dates back to Edward the Black Prince (1330-1376).

✱ Charles was the longest serving (so far), Prince of Wales.

WILLIAM, P.O.W SINCE 2022

ACTION MAN!

Having made it through school and college, royal tradition dictated that Charles should serve time in the Armed Forces. To everyone's surprise, he threw himself into his new jobs

HELICOPTER PILOT

In Autumn 1974, Charles completed a helicopter conversion course and then joined the commando carrier HMS *Hermes*, as a helicopter pilot in the Fleet Air Arm.

He was assigned two Wessex choppers, painted bright red on the nose and tail to mark them out as 'royal.'

Charles was not allowed to fly Wasps or any other single-engine copters because they had a poor safety record - which, as he pointed out, begged the question:

'WHY WERE THE OTHER PILOTS ALLOWED TO FLY THEM?'

The Prince flew for 500 hours in total. At one point, Charles was told off by the Commander of the ship for 'showing off' as he flew crates of beer on to *Hermes*!

When his time on-board came to an end, he said, 'I had more fun flying than I had ever had before.'

PILOT & OFFICER

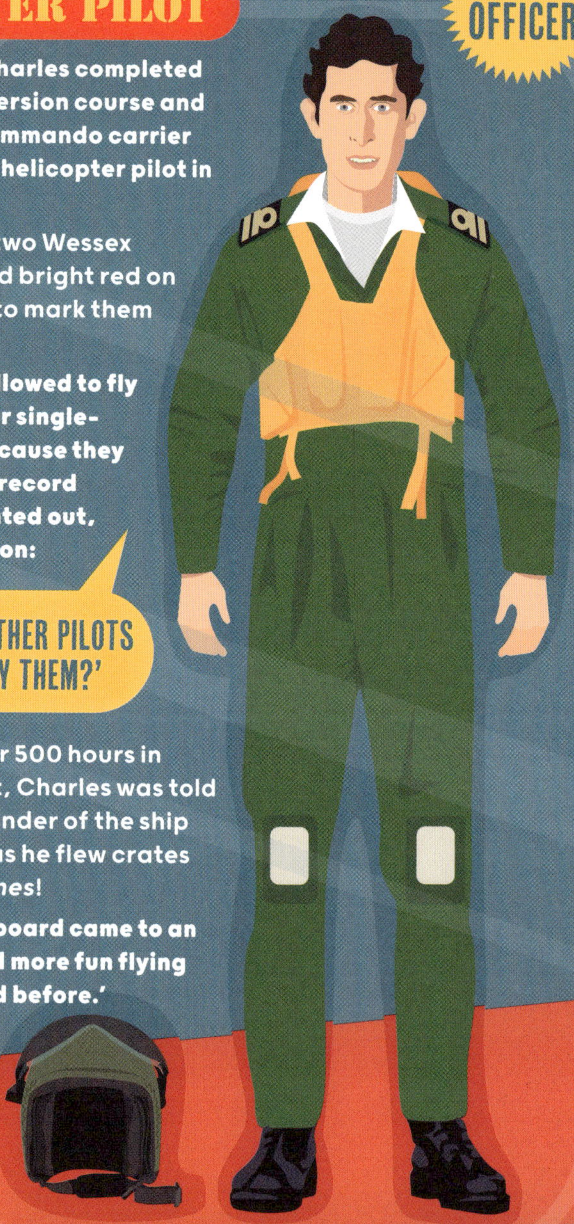

CHARLES FLEW FOR A TOTAL OF 500 HOURS

RAF JET PILOT

In March 1971, Charles joined the Royal Air Force for five months to earn his wings and qualify as a jet pilot. He obtained his RAF wings as Flight Lieutenant Wales in August of that year.

After eight hours of training Charles was allowed to fly solo. He said, 'The feeling of power, smooth, unworried power, is incredible.'

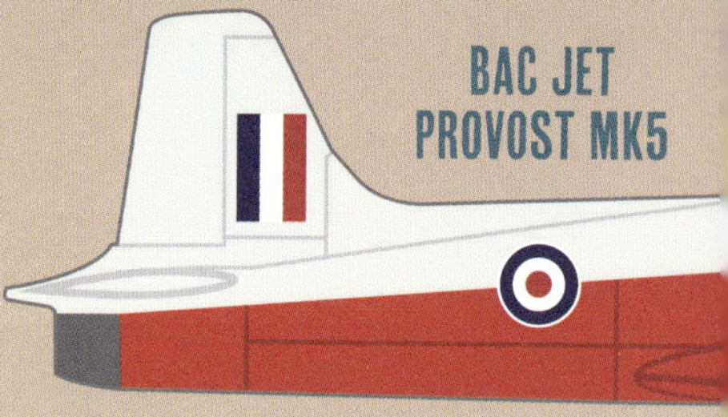

BAC JET PROVOST MK5

NAVAL OFFICER

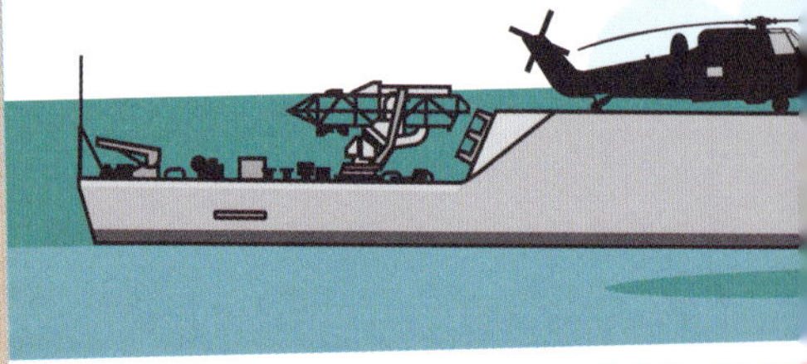

Charles's father (Prince Philip), grandfather (George VI) and two great grandfathers (George V and Prince Louis of Battenberg) all served in the Royal Navy.

His mentor, his great uncle Lord Mountbatten (aka Uncle Dickie), who Charles called his 'honorary grandfather', and Prince Philip were both keen on him going to sea.

Acting Sub Lieutenant Prince Charles joined the Navy in September 1971.

Charles made his first parachute jump in July 1971. When he was appointed Colonel-in-Chief of the Parachute Regiment six years later, he insisted on taking its parachute training course.

Charles said…

'I DIDN'T THINK I COULD LOOK THEM IN THE EYE… UNLESS I'D DONE THE COURSE'

MINEHUNTER!

Charles's most 'terrifying' time during five years in the Navy was as Commander of minehunter HMS *Bronington* in 1976.

The *Bronington*'s anchor became caught on a telecommunications cable that linked Ireland with the British mainland! Charles decided to leave the anchor behind…

HORSEMAN

An extremely keen polo player until he retired from the game in 2005, Charles also rode in a professional horserace at Ludlow in 1980, in which he finished second.

HMS NORFOLK

D 21

'I REALLY HATE MISSING AN ENGLISH SUMMER. IT IS ALWAYS SPECIAL… EACH TIME IT IS NEW AND ORIGINAL…'

Learnt **MORSE CODE**

Passed **DIVING TESTS**

Got into **SURFING**

After training and a bit of surfing, he joined the crew of the destroyer HMS *Norfolk* in Gibraltar.

For the next nine months, he trained for his Bridge Watchkeeping Certificate, the qualification needed to take charge of a ship.

In a letter to Uncle Dickie, Charles said, 'I stumble around the ship, falling down hatches and striking my head against bulkheads in an effort to find my way about.' But he eventually found his feet.

He also served on HMS *Churchill*, a nuclear submarine that he was allowed to drive, or, to use the proper term, 'fly'.

He later joined the frigate HMS *Minerva* for eight months in the Caribbean. In that time, he attended 40 to 50 cocktail parties, but became very homesick.

THE ROYAL DRAWING SCHOOL
A keen amateur painter, Charles founded The Prince's Drawing School in 2000. It was renamed the Royal Drawing School in 2014 and remains a place where expert teachers help students explore their creativity.

THE PRINCE'S COUNTRYSIDE FUND
Founded in 2010, this fund supports family farms and rural communities. Fifteen years later, around £10 million had been invested in more than 400 projects.

A NEW

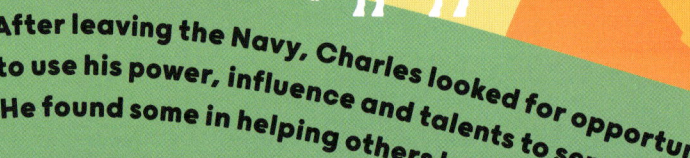

After leaving the Navy, Charles looked for opportunities to use his power, influence and talents to serve his country. He found some in helping others less fortunate

THE KING'S TRUST

During the mid-1970s, there were record levels of youth unemployment and 'juvenile' crime was on the rise. This and the stories he heard firsthand, led Charles to believe many young people were being left behind.

It's said, that in 1976 the Prince used his Navy severance pay of £7,400 to fund 21 pilot projects that in different ways all aimed to help young Britons create a better future for themselves.

These early projects were set up all over the United Kingdom and included funding for an East London social centre, a fishing club, training for young lifeguards and a bicycle repair scheme.

They were the beginning of The Prince's Trust (renamed The King's Trust in 2024), Charles's charity with a mission to help young, disadvantaged people boost their confidence, find a job or start a business.

The Prince wanted the Trust to be about 'challenge' and 'adventure' and allow him to meet people in 'less artificial circumstances', than a royal visit.

IN SEPTEMBER 2020, THE TRUST CELEBRATED HAVING HELPED
1 MILLION
YOUNG PEOPLE TRANSFORM THEIR LIVES

DUMFRIES HOUSE
Charles resurrected this 18th century Scottish property. Now open to the public, it also offers training opportunities to young people looking to learn traditional skills and crafts.

LIFE!

CORONATION FOOD PROJECT
In 2023, the King founded Coronation Food Project which aims to reduce waste and hunger by redistributing surplus food from supermarkets and restaurants to the many people who cannot afford to buy it.

In its first year, the project redirected **940 TONNES** of food and provided **2.24 MILLION MEALS**

18 NUMBER OF CHARITIES CHARLES HAS FOUNDED

400+ NUMBER OF ORGANISATIONS OF WHICH CHARLES HAS BEEN PATRON OR PRESIDENT

Magician **DYNAMO**

AMONG THE MANY SUCCESS STORIES...
Big stars that received the Trust's help early in their careers

Rock bands **MUSE, ELBOW, STEREOPHONICS**

Award-winning actors

DAVID OYELOWO | IDRIS ELBA

TRUNKIS!
Rob Law, the entrepreneur behind Trunki ride-on kids' suitcases, was awarded a grant in the company's early days. He went on to sell more than five million cases worldwide!

ROYAL GREEN

Decades before climate change became a mainstream issue, Charles was calling for action and championing sustainability

As children, Charles and his sister Anne had their own **VEGETABLE PATCH** at Buckingham Palace.

> **I REMEMBER YEARS AGO, IN THE '60S, WHEN I WAS A TEENAGER, MINDING SO MUCH ABOUT ALL THE THINGS THAT WERE GOING ON, THE DESTRUCTION OF EVERYTHING.... THIS COMPLETE DETERMINATION, SOMEHOW, TO DEFEAT NATURE**

1970s

★ In February 1970… Charles, then 21, made a speech warning of the dangers of plastic waste and *'the horrifying effects of pollution in all its cancerous forms'*.

★ Over the years since, he has highlighted the growing problems of climate change and deforestation and has promoted sustainability in soil, water, forests and fish stocks.

2000s

THE HARMONY SUMMIT

The King's Foundation, established in 1990, supports the growth of sustainable communities around the world.

In July 2025, the foundation hosted the first Harmony Summit at Highgrove.

Community leaders, environmentalists, activists, farmers, herbalists, crafts people, philanthropists and the King attended to celebrate 'harmony with nature'.

A fire ceremony took place within a ring of flowers. A conch shell was blown, and attendees reached to the sky and gave thanks.

1990s

TV CAMPAIGNER

By 1990, green issues were receiving serious attention and that year Charles made a TV documentary on the future of the planet called *The Earth in Balance*.

Charles's favourite car is an Aston Martin DB6 Mark 2 Volante.

A 21st birthday gift from his parents, it has been converted so it runs on surplus white wine and whey, a by-product of cheese-making.

1980s

In 1980, Charles set up a **BOTTLE BANK** for Buckingham Palace.

HIGHGROVE

★ After making Highgrove House his home in 1980, Charles made its gardens **ORGANIC** and **SUSTAINABLE**.

★ He installed an organic sewage system that used a **REED BED** to absorb waste and a pond where **PURIFIED WATER** gathers before running off into the nearby river. The estate's land also includes four acres of **WILDFLOWER MEADOWS**.

★ In 1981, Charles **BORROWED TWO COWS** from the Queen to provide milk for Highgrove and by the mid-1980s was looking to set up an **ORGANIC FARM**.

NOT SO SILLY, AFTER ALL...?

In a 1986 interview, when asked what he did in his garden Charles said:

> ❝ I JUST COME AND TALK TO THE PLANTS, REALLY – VERY IMPORTANT TO TALK TO THEM, THEY RESPOND ❞

He was widely mocked for what was seen as a peculiar habit but many gardeners do this too.

Also, a 2007 study by scientists in South Korea suggested classical music may have had a positive effect on the growth of rice plants, and other research has shown evidence of trees and plants communicating with each other.

In short, Charles may be on to something...

> ❝ I HAVE PUT MY HEART AND SOUL INTO HIGHGROVE' CHARLES HAS WRITTEN. 'ALL THE THINGS I HAVE TRIED TO DO IN THIS SMALL CORNER OF GLOUCESTER HAVE BEEN THE PHYSICAL EXPRESSION OF A PERSONAL PHILOSOPHY ❞

HUSBAND & FATHER

Deciding who to marry is a big decision for anyone but for Charles, as heir to the British throne, it had a whole heap of extra complications…

Love & Marriage

MONTHLY

50 pence

WATCHED BY 750 MILLION

CHARLES & DIANA
MARRIED 29TH JULY 1981

Royal wedding

WHY LADY DI?

AN ARISTOCRAT As a daughter of Earl Spencer and Frances Shand Kydd, Diana was descended from Charles II on both sides of the family.

NOT A CATHOLIC The Act of Settlement (1701) forbid Charles from marrying a Catholic.

NO PREVIOUS RELATIONSHIP Diana had no exes who might have had embarrassing stories from her past.

A fairy-tale beginning

- On 29 July 1981, Charles, then 32 years old, married Lady Diana Spencer, aged just 20. An estimated worldwide TV audience of 750 million watched the wedding.
- The couple had first met four years earlier, when Charles was dating Diana's eldest sister, Sarah.
- There were fireworks and a concert the night before, beacons and bonfires throughout the country, and hundreds of items of 'commemorabilia' (souvenirs such as mugs, plates and tea towels).
- Conducting the ceremony, the Archbishop of Canterbury said, '…this is the stuff of which fairy tales are made…'.

THE BOYS

WILLIAM & HARRY

WILLIAM ARTHUR PHILIP LOUIS was born on 21 June 1982. He was the first royal baby to be born in a hospital. Prince William is now Prince of Wales and heir to the throne.

HENRY CHARLES ALBERT DAVID, now known as Prince Harry, Duke of Sussex, was born 15 September 1984. He is fifth in line to the throne after William and his three children.

DIANA

THE MODERN ROYAL!

EXCLUSIVE

Queen of hearts

NOT AFRAID TO SHOW EMOTION!

As **PRINCESS OF WALES**, Diana was hugely popular and quickly became one of the most famous people in the world.

She was seen as a new, modern kind of royal who was at ease with all kinds of people and not afraid to show emotion.

In a 1995 TV interview, Diana said she would like to be thought of as the 'queen of people's hearts'.

A TRAGIC ENDING

Sadly, Diana found the constant attention and pressure of being a royal difficult to live with.

Also, Charles was in love with another woman. The couple separated in 1992 and divorced in 1996. Tragically, just a year later, in August 1997, Diana died in a car crash in Paris.

The UK's prime minister Tony Blair described her as 'The People's Princess.' Around two billion people watched Diana's funeral on television.

Royals are usually wealthy, and Charles is certainly that. Here's where his money comes from...

HOW RICH IS THE KING?

£132 MILLION
PER YEAR 2025 - 2027

SOVEREIGN GRANT

This is money provided by British taxpayers and given by the government to the King and his family every year.

It goes towards the cost of their royal duties, maintaining palaces and paying staff. The Sovereign Grant for 2025 to 2027 is £132 million per year.

£369M COST OF A 10-YEAR REFURBISHMENT OF BUCKINGHAM PALACE

PROFITS

ASSETS WORTH £15.5 BILLION

615,000 ACRES

CROWN ESTATE

This is land and property that belongs to the British monarchy - not Charles personally - that is managed as a business on behalf of the country. Any profit made from the estate goes to the government.

The Crown Estate has around 615,000 acres of land that has been estimated to be worth a colossal £15.5bn.

It owns farmland, shoreline and shops including the whole of Regent Street in the middle of London.

£1.1BN MADE FROM OFFSHORE WINDFARMS 2024 - 2025

DUCHIES

The King and his heir also receive **private incomes** from the profit generated by their duchies.

Most of their land was seized by kings in the centuries after the Norman Conquest of 1066.

DUCHY OF LANCASTER

Inherited from his mother and now owned by King Charles III.

45,000 ACRES
IN ENGLAND & WALES

2024 – 2025, the Duchy of Lancaster made **£24.4 million**

ART, JEWELLERY and other valuable items

The royal family also owns private estates including Sandringham and Balmoral.

DUCHY OF CORNWALL

- The Duchy of Cornwall estate has provided Charles with his own private income since he was 18.
- The Duchy was created by King Edward III in 1337 for his son, Edward the Black Prince.

LARGEST PRIVATE LANDOWNER IN ENGLAND
135,000 ACRES

- FARMLAND
- COASTLINE
- FORESTS
- RIVERS
- FLATS & HOUSES
- THE OVAL STADIUM

CHARGES RENTS
- BUSINESSES
- PRISONS
- ARMED FORCES
- PORTS

£22.9 MILLION
2024-2025

GLORIOUS FOOD
During Charles's time in charge the Duchy became famous for a line of organic food products.

He established the Duchy Originals (now Duchy Organic) in 1990 and its first product was a box of biscuits.

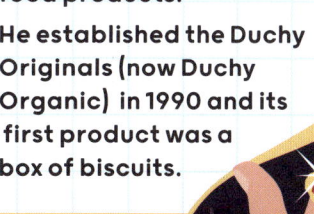

PASS THE DUCHY
After he became King in 2023, Charles passed the Duchy on to William.

DOWN WITH CARBUNCLES!

In general, British royals avoid expressing personal opinions in public but Charles is one family member who has always had plenty to say about subjects close to his heart – and buildings and architecture in particular

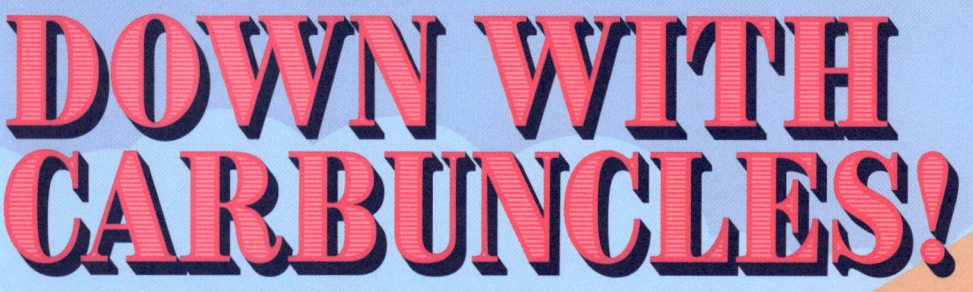

'Monstrous!'

In 1984, Charles made a now famous speech in which he described a planned extension to London's National Gallery as 'a monstrous carbuncle on the face of a much-loved and elegant friend'.

So began decades of conflict and rivalry between Charles and architects who worked in modern styles.

His comments included describing Birmingham's city centre 'a monstrous concrete maze', with a library that resembled 'a place where books are incinerated, not kept'.

Charles felt the tower blocks and other concrete developments of the 1960s and 1970s had a negative effect on people's lives and communities.

BIRMINGHAM CENTRAL LIBRARY 1973-2016

PLANNED (BUT NEVER BUILT) EXTENSION TO NATIONAL GALLERY

"MY VISION OF BRITAIN IS..."

In 1988 and 1989, Charles put forward his ideas in a book and a TV show, both called *A Vision of Britain*, and in 1990 founded the Prince of Wales' Institute of Architecture where architects of the future were trained.

The New York Times

Charles championed more traditional design and materials. The New York Times called him...

'THE MOST PROMINENT ARCHITECTURE CRITIC IN THE WORLD'

WELCOME TO POUNDBURY
POPULATION 4,000

In 1993, building work began on Poundbury. This small Dorset town was built under Charles's direction on 400 acres he owned as part of the Duchy of Cornwall.

True to Charles's design ideas and commitment to sustainability, Poundbury is a mix of squares, streets, homes, shops and factories. Its cottages and houses include classic features such as cupolas, pillars and pointy roofs.

Three decades later, Poundbury has more than 4,000 residents and another 2,000 people work in the area.

NANSLEDAN
Please drive with care

Nansledan is an extension of the Cornish town of Newquay, also built in line with Charles's vision.

Work on the housing development began in 2014, using local materials and providing training for people in building skills. By 2025, 840 houses had been built with plans for another 2,860 in place.

Queen Camilla

```
MAJOR BRUCE SHAND ─┬─ ROSALIND CUBITT
                   │
      ┌────────────┼────────────┐
   ANNABEL      CAMILLA        MARK
KING CHARLES III ─┘    └─ ANDREW PARKER BOWLES
                           │
                    ┌──────┴──────┐
              TOM PARKER      LAURA PARKER
                BOWLES           BOWLES
```

It's a girl!

Camilla Rosemary Shand was born on **17 JULY 1947** in London

Growing up, 'Milla', as she was known, was an outgoing tomboy, and the oldest of the three children of Major Bruce Shand, a wine merchant, and Rosalind Cubitt.

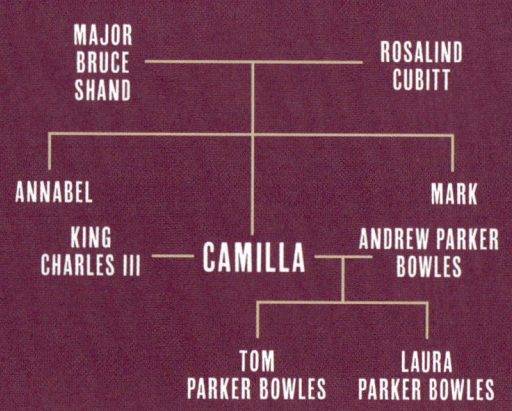

She met Charles, then 21, at a polo match in 1970 and they dated for a short time. He called their relationship, **'BLISSFUL, PEACEFUL AND MUTUALLY HAPPY…'**

Education

She went to Dumbrells school, East Sussex, and Queen's Gate in London, where she passed one O-level and showed a talent for fencing.

Marriage 1

However, Camilla, 23, was in an on-off relationship with army officer **ANDREW PARKER BOWLES** and in 1973 she married him while Charles was away with the Navy.

Why did they marry other people?

The short answer is **old-fashioned attitudes** and **snobbery**

- THOUGHT TOO YOUNG FOR CAMILLA
- OKAY FOR HIM TO HAVE DATED BEFORE 
- NOT ARISTOCRATIC ENOUGH
- HAD DATED SEVERAL OTHER PEOPLE

Charles has known his wife for over 50 years, and their love has endured throughout difficult times and intense scrutiny

Becoming Queen

1981

Camilla attended Charles and Diana's wedding in 1981. Later, Diana famously said, 'There were three of us in the marriage - it was rather crowded.'

1986

Charles and Camilla are said to have re-started their romantic relationship in 1986 after his marriage had 'broken down.'

1999

In 1999, two years after Diana died, Charles and Camilla made their first public appearance as a couple.

2005

On marrying Charles in 2005, Camilla officially became Princess of Wales but chose the title HRH Duchess of Cornwall instead.

2022

In 2022, Queen Elizabeth II expressed her 'sincere wish' that Camilla becomes Queen Consort when Charles becomes king.

2023

Camilla was crowned Queen Consort at Charles's coronation the following year, and she is now addressed as Queen Camilla.

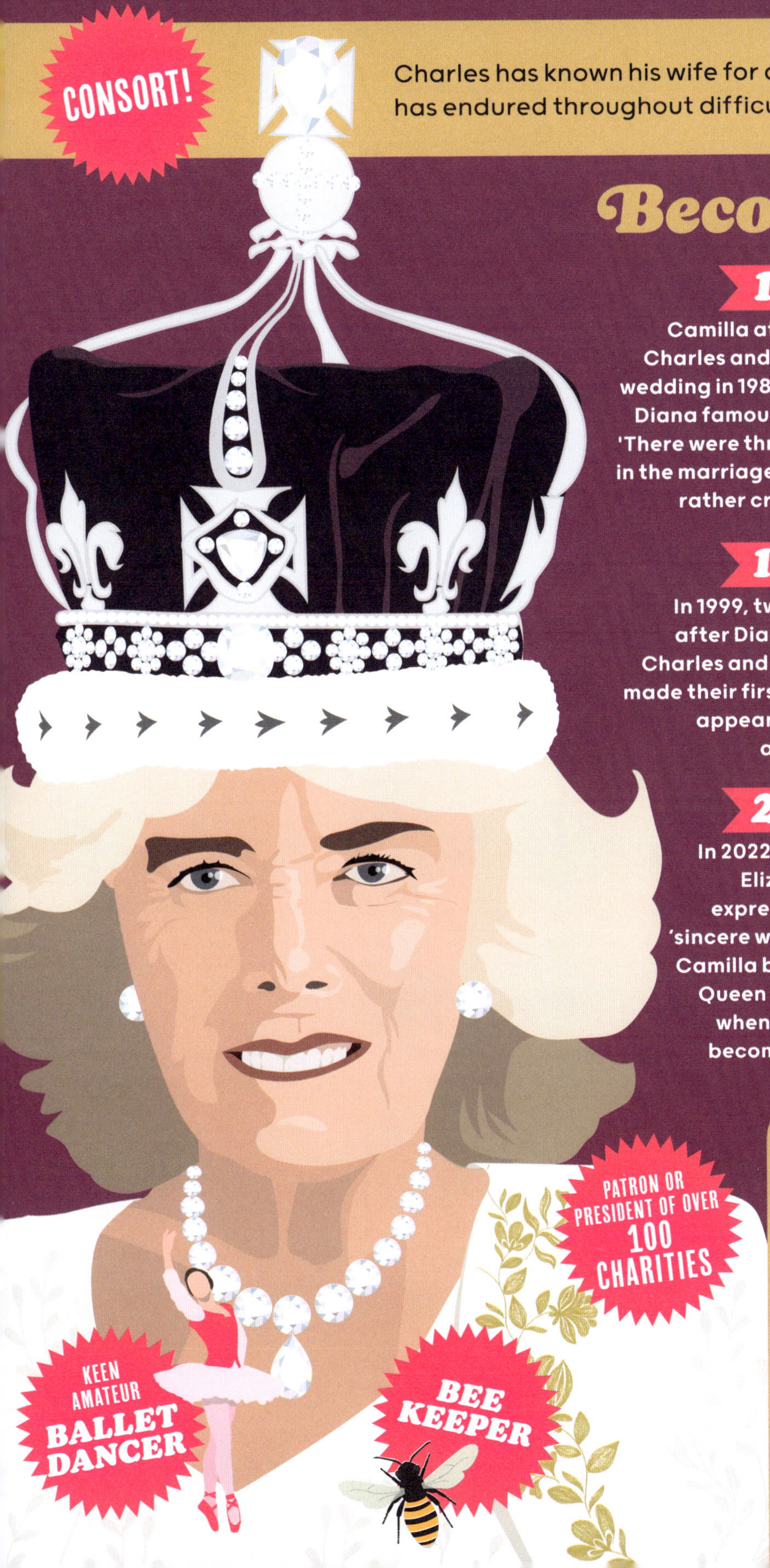
CONSORT!
PATRON OR PRESIDENT OF OVER 100 CHARITIES
KEEN AMATEUR BALLET DANCER
BEE KEEPER

FANCY BEING MY CONSORT?

The person married to a British monarch is crowned a Prince or Queen Consort as part of their partner's coronation.

That applied to Queen Elizabeth II's mother, Elizabeth, and grandmother, Mary.

However, it's not always the case, and there is no law that applies to that title.

WELL AND TRULY CULTURED!

As a boy, his grandmother, the Queen Mother, encouraged Charles's interest in music and art. The King's passion for anything creative has been life-long and varied…

Painter

Throughout his life, the King has been a keen painter with a preference for watercolours. In 1987, he submitted, anonymously, a painting to the Royal Academy and it was selected for the Summer Exhibition of that year.

'PAINTING… REFRESHES PARTS OF THE SOUL WHICH OTHER ACTIVITIES CAN'T REACH.'
Charles III

Has authored or contributed to **30 BOOKS**

BEST-SELLING AUTHOR

The King has written, or contributed to, over 30 books so far but the best known remains his 1980 children's book, *The Old Man of Lochnagar*.

Based on stories he told his brothers and sisters when they were young, it's about the adventures of an old man who lives in caves by the loch below Lochnagar, a mountain that overlooks Balmoral.

Charles has read English, Welsh and Gaelic versions of the book for TV, and it has been adapted as a stage play and a ballet.

THE OLD MAN OF LOCHNAGAR — HRH The Prince of Wales

STAGE PLAY   BALLET

Magician

In 1975, Charles passed an audition to become a member of the renowned society of stage magicians, the Magic Circle.

Soap star

Charles made a brief appearance on ITV's **CORONATION STREET** in 2000, and to mark Queen Elizabeth II's Platinum Jubilee he and Camilla attended a street party in the BBC's **EASTENDERS**.

On a visit to TV studios in 2012, Charles presented BBC Scotland's **WEATHER FORECAST**.

Comedy

Charles has the most serious of jobs, but he does enjoy a laugh.
He was a huge fan of *The Goon Show*, a 1950s radio comedy show that starred Spike Milligan, Peter Sellers, Harry Secombe and Michael Bentine who all became Charles's friends.

At school and university, Charles loved to act. He also co-starred with Sir Stephen Fry and Sir Roger Moore in a comedy sketch for a 1998 Prince's Trust concert.
In 2012, he appeared in a sketch alongside Dame Judi Dench, Sir Ian McKellen and others at the Royal Shakespeare Company.

'TO BE, OR NOT TO BE, THAT IS THE QUESTION...'

Music

King Charles III is a passionate classical music fan, but the 2025 publication of his Commonwealth Day pop playlist was something of a surprise.

His 17 selections included...

'THE LOCOMOTION' Kylie Minogue

'CRAZY IN LOVE' Beyoncé

Could You be Loved
BOB MARLEY & THE WAILERS

The King met Bob Marley when he came to London in the 1970s and remembers, 'that marvellous, infectious energy he had but also his deep sincerity, and his profound concern for his community'.

'I always recall his words: **"THE PEOPLE HAVE A VOICE INSIDE OF THEM"** He gave the world that voice in a way that no one who heard can ever forget.'

BOB MARLEY

BEYONCÉ

CORONATION FEATS

Following the death of his 'darling Mama' in May 2023, Charles ascended the British throne and was crowned in a ceremony rich in history, but which also included some notable firsts

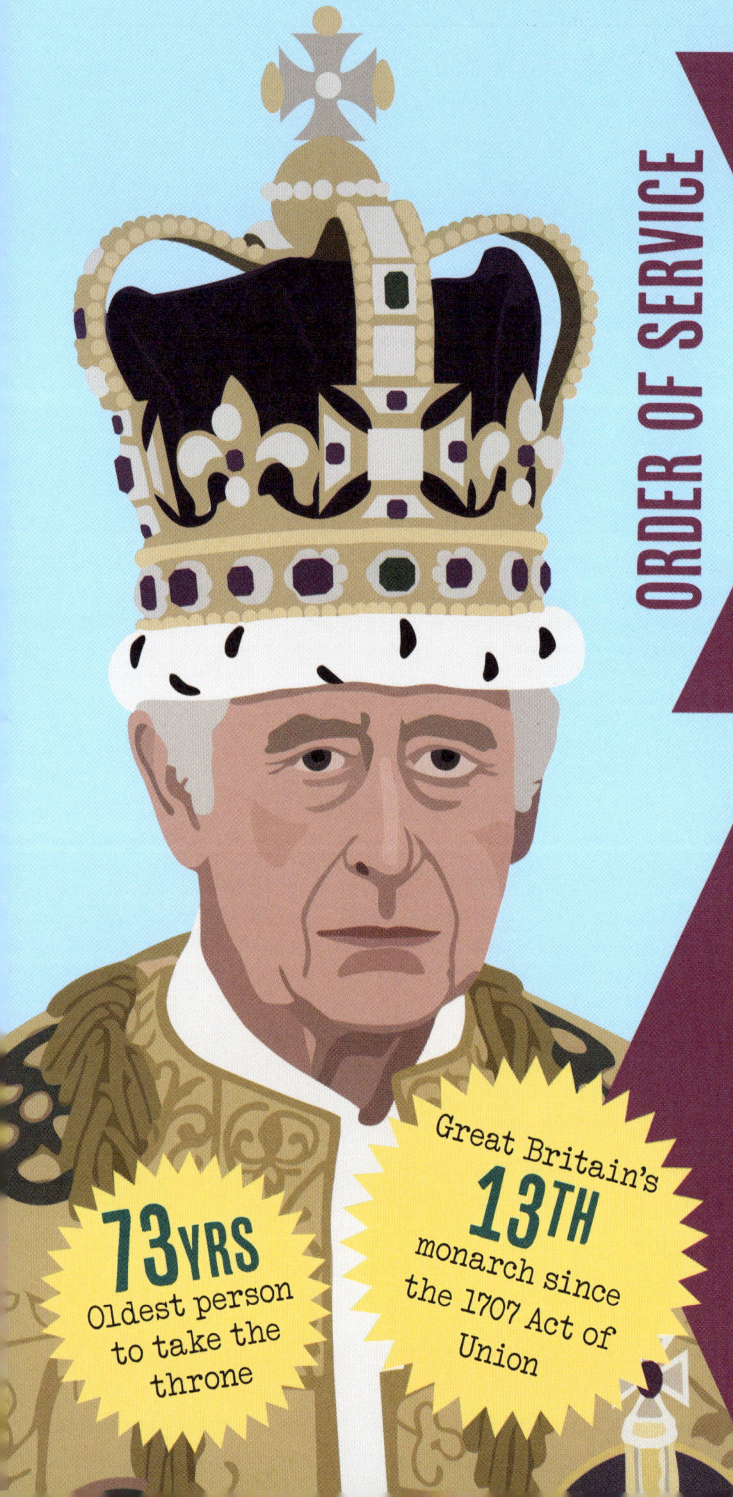
73YRS
Oldest person to take the throne
Great Britain's
13TH
monarch since the 1707 Act of Union

ORDER OF SERVICE

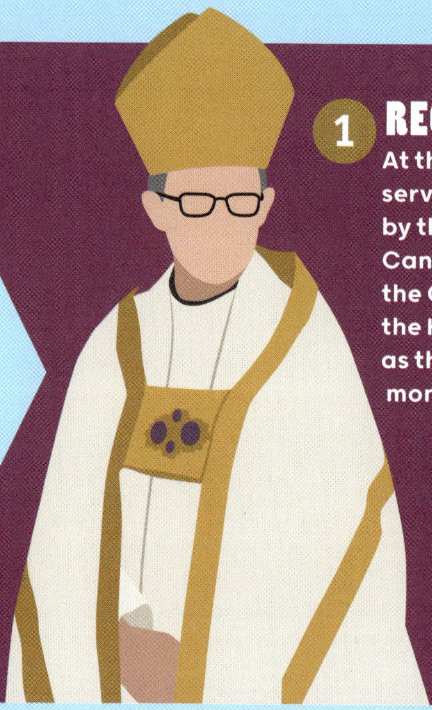

1 RECOGNITION

At the start of the service conducted by the Archbishop of Canterbury (leader of the Church of England the King is recognised as the true 'undoubted monarch.

6 ENTHRONEMENT AND HOMAGE

The King moves to the throne to receive The Homage, a promise of allegiance from the Archbishop of Canterbury; his heir, the Prince of Wales; and the congregation. The Queen Consort is then anointed and crowned and takes her place alongside the King.

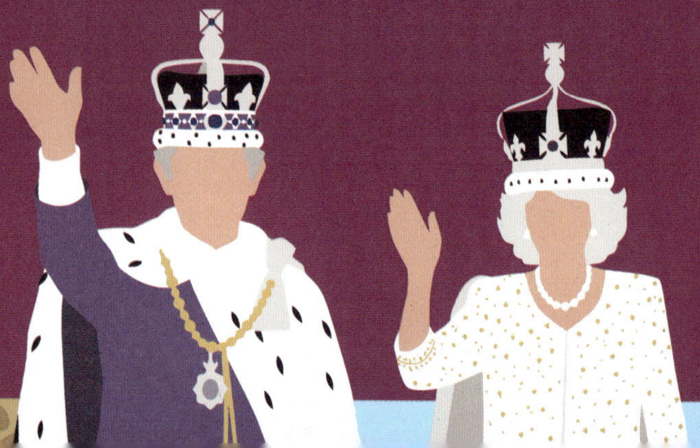

CROWNED
6 MAY 2023
IN
WESTMINSTER ABBEY

40 sovereigns crowned here

Venue for every coronation since Christmas Day **1066**

2 THE OATH
The King promises to rule according to the country's laws and customs. The oath is a series of questions answered by the monarch. To reflect his interest in religions other than Christianity, Charles's oath included a new part which stated the Church of England…

'…WILL SEEK TO FOSTER AN ENVIRONMENT WHERE PEOPLE OF ALL FAITHS AND BELIEFS MAY LIVE FREELY'

ANOINTING SPOON **700 YEARS OLD**

3 ANOINTING
Also called the consecration, this is said to be the most sacred part of the ceremony. Behind a screen, the King sits in the Coronation Chair, and the Archbishop pours 'holy oil' on his hands, chest and head using a 700-year-old spoon.

The recipe for the oil is **SECRET**

5 CROWNING
The King sits on the Coronation Chair, and the Archbishop places the St Edward's Crown on his head. This crown is only used for this part of a coronation.

4 INVESTITURE
The King is presented with items that have special significance…

SWORD OF OFFERING

SPURS

ARMILLS (bracelets)

ORB

SOVEREIGN'S RINGS

SCEPTRE WITH CROSS

SCEPTRE WITH DOVE

CHARLOTTE
LILIBET
GEORGE
LOUIS

KING & GRANDPA

At an age when many people are retired and taking it easy, King Charles took on one of the biggest jobs in the world and he is also a very active grandpa

Dearest Grandpa

In 2013, Charles became a grandfather for the first time when Prince George was born. The eldest child of William and his wife Kate, George now has a sister, Princess Charlotte born in 2015, and a brother, Prince Louis born in 2018.
Harry and his wife Meghan, had Prince Archie in 2019 and Princess Lilibet in 2021.
Queen Camilla has said Charles…

> '…WILL GET DOWN ON HIS KNEES AND CRAWL ABOUT WITH THEM FOR HOURS, MAKING FUNNY NOISES AND LAUGHING.'

ARCHIE

AND WHAT DO YOU DO?

As King, Charles is…
HEAD OF STATE OF THE UNITED KINGDOM
(ENGLAND, WALES, SCOTLAND & NORTHERN IRELAND)

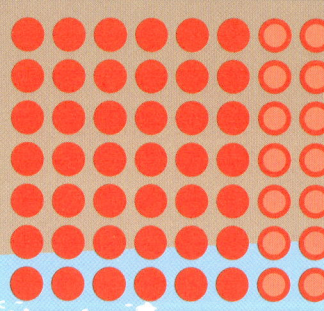

HEAD OF THE COMMONWEALTH

HEAD OF STATE

56 COUNTRIES
2.5 BILLION PEOPLE

Most of the **POWER** Charles has is **SYMBOLIC** and **CEREMONIAL**

MAP OF COMMONWEALTH COUNTRIES

HIS MAJESTY'S GOVERNMENT

RED DESPATCH BOX

- **The King has no official say in what the British government does** but receives daily updates from the government, delivered in red leather boxes.
- These include details of important meetings and documents that need his signature.

THE KING'S OFFICIAL LOGO

THE KING

OFFICIAL TASKS

APPOINTING A GOVERNMENT
The leader of the party that wins a general election goes to Buckingham Palace, where the King invites him or her to form a government.

DISSOLVING PARLIAMENT
The King also dissolves (closes) Parliament before a general election.

THE KING'S SPEECH
At the State Opening of a new parliament after a general election, the King's Speech, outlining the new government's plans, is given from a throne in the House of Lords.

ROYAL APPROVAL
All parliament's legislation (plans for new laws) must be given Royal Assent (approved) by the King.

MEET THE P.M. AT THE PALACE

The Prime Minister normally meets the King in private every Wednesday at Buckingham Palace.

OTHER DUTIES

The King's **BIRTHDAY HONOURS** are titles awarded every June by the monarch to people who have done exceptional things.

The King and Queen are also patrons of charities, many of which are linked to their personal interests.

In November, the King attends the annual **REMEMBRANCE CEREMONY** at the Cenotaph in London. The event honours those that served and died during conflicts involving British and Commonwealth Armed Forces.

Charles plays host to visiting heads of state, ambassadors and other officials, and visits other countries.

372 ROYAL ENGAGEMENTS IN 2024

GLOSSARY

ABDICATION
Act of renouncing or giving up the throne.

ANOINTMENT
Application of oil to a person or object during a religious ceremony.

BRITISH EMPIRE
The collective name of the territories ruled by the British between the late 16th century and the late 20th century.

CARBUNCLE
A cluster of boils on the skin.

CLIMATE CHANGE
The ongoing increase in the Earth's temperature and its effects.

COMMONWEALTH
An association of 56 countries created in 1949.

CONSORT
The wife or husband of a reigning queen or king.

DUCHY
The territory owned by a duke or duchess.

HEIR
The person entitled to the property and rank of another after that person's death.

INDIGENOUS PEOPLES
Communities with long-held ancestral ties to a particular area of land and its resources.

JUBILEE
A celebration marking a significant anniversary during a monarch's reign.

ORGANIC
Food produced without the use of artificial chemicals.

PATRON
Honorary role in an organisation taken by an influential person.

POLO
A team sport in which players on horseback use long mallets to hit a ball and score a goal.

PRINCIPALITY
A territory ruled by a prince or princess.

REPUBLIC
A country in which power lies with those elected by the public, not a king or queen and his or her family.

SUSTAINABILITY
Looking after resources, of the environment in particular.

TRUST
An organisation in which trustees manage assets for the benefit of others.

WHEY
A by-product of the cheese-making process, used to fuel Charles III's sports car.

WINGS
Badge worn by pilots in Britain's Royal Air Force that shows they have completed training.

First published 2026 by Button Books, an imprint of Guild of Master Craftsman Publications Ltd, Castle Place, 166 High Street, Lewes, East Sussex, BN7 1XU, UK. Copyright in the Work © GMC Publications Ltd, 2026. ISBN 9781787081871. Distributed by Publishers Group West in the United States. All rights reserved. No part of this publication may be reproduced, stored in a retrieval system, or transmitted in any form or by any means without the prior permission of the publisher and copyright owner. While every effort has been made to obtain permission from the copyright holders for all material used in this book, the publishers will be pleased to hear from anyone who has not been appropriately acknowledged and to make the correction in future reprints. The publishers and authors can accept no legal responsibility for any consequences arising from the application of information, advice, or instructions given in this publication. A catalogue record for this book is available from the British Library. Words: Robert Hiley Editorial: Jonathan Harwood, Jane Roe, Anne Guillot Design: Tim Lambert Illustrations: Alex Bailey, Matt Carr, Shutterstock. Colour origination by GMC Reprographics. Printed and bound in China.